Healing Our Anger

Healing Our Anger

Frank West

Library of Congress Control Number: 2010906277
ISBN: Hardcover   978-1-4500-9552-5
                 Softcover   978-1-4500-9551-8
                 Ebook   978-1-4500-9553-2

This book was printed in the United States of America.

To order additional copies of this book, contact:
Xlibris Corporation
1-888-795-4274
www.Xlibris.com
Orders@Xlibris.com
79334

Healing Our Anger

Contents

Preface..9

Acknowledgment...11

1. Beginning...17
2. Eight Psychological Truths about Anger.................20
3. The Geography of the Mind...............................33
4. Two Stories—East and West 40
5. Questions and Answers.....................................50
6. Benediction 68

I dedicate this work to my beloved wife, Martha, now deceased, who taught me the meaning of love. She has been and still remains my collaborator, inspiration, and guide, patiently and gently leading me toward a clearer vision of the Truth.

Frank West
Guilford, Connecticut
Autumn 2009

Preface

This little volume is the first of a series of three that deal with key ideas found in the spiritual/psychological writings scribed by Dr. Helen Schucman more than a generation ago and known as *A Course in Miracles*. The ideas as I treat them here are grounded in my own personal experiences of a lifetime that (so far) has lasted over eighty-three years.

Acknowledgment

I'm grateful for the thoughtful editing of this work by my friend Chad Hardin, musician, composer, and master of the written word. Without his efforts—or his sure feel for the tone and cadence of my particular voice—this book could not have come to be.

The text that follows is an edited transcription that combines two workshops presented in 2009 by Frank West entitled "Healing Our Anger." The first talk occurred on June 3 at RJ Julia Bookseller in Madison, Connecticut; the second on June 13 at the Mountain Meadows Community in Ashland, Oregon.

A Note on Annotations

Most of the references and quotations in *Healing Our Anger* are taken from *A Course in Miracles*. The *Course* consists of a Text, a Workbook for Students, a Manual for Teachers, and two supplemental pamphlets—*Psychotherapy: Purpose, Process and Practice* and *The Song of Prayer*.

Abbreviations are used as follows:

T: Text		Intro:	Introduction
W: Workbook for Students		P:	*Psychotherapy: Purpose, Process and Practice*
M: Manual for Teachers		S:	*The Song of Prayer*

Taking (*T-26.IV.4:7*) as an example of an annotation referencing *A Course in Miracles*, *T* stands for Text, *26* is the chapter number, the roman numeral *IV* is the section within the chapter, *4* is the paragraph number of that section, and *7* is the sentence number within the paragraph.

In some of the quotations, I have taken the liberty of changing pronouns at editors' requests.

Chapter 1

Beginning

I woke up this morning and I realized it was June 3, my wedding anniversary. And if my wife, Martha, who died four years ago last Monday, were here, I actually wouldn't be talking to you tonight—I'd be out in the town with her, dining and dancing! Today would have been our fifty-ninth year of marriage, and I dedicate this evening to her.

Martha was my best teacher, and she taught me about love, which I knew nothing about when I married her. I'm so grateful for her life, and so I want to share what she has helped me learn and pass it on to you.

Before I go on, I'd like to find out how many of you have any awareness of what *A Course in Miracles* is. (*Counting the raised hands*) 1, 2, 3 . . . only four of you. Good! I'm so glad most of you don't know the Course because that gives me the opportunity to help you learn what it is. For me it's been a great blessing. My wife, Martha, introduced me to it, of course. It has helped me make sense of my life, which has been a long one—over eighty years. I've written the story of my life in my book, which is called *From Guilt to the Gift of Miracles*. A miracle, as defined by the Course, happens in that moment "When an ancient hate is changed to a current love." The subtitle of my book is *A Memoir of Mistakes*

Mended. I've had a lifetime of mistakes, and I write about some of them in my book and show as well how I've learned to mend those mistakes, through the healing the miracle offers. And at the bottom of the front cover of my book I've written as epigram one of my favorite quotes from the Course: "If you knew Who walks beside you on the way you have chosen, fear would be impossible."

Now, why had I written this book? I had no interest in writing a book, except I'd become a close friend of Ken Wapnick, whose name some of you are acquainted with, I'm sure, and who has been one of the principal teachers of *A Course in Miracles* for several decades now. He's been my mentor and now my friend. What Ken would say to me every time we met was, "Frank, why don't you write?" He kept saying that, so I finally said, "Well, but what would I write about?" He said, "Write about your life!" And so, because I knew he loved me, I decided to take that seriously and go ahead and do it, and that's what this book is.

And I promise you, I'm not going to read from my book! I've been to lectures/booksignings like this, and often the presenter just reads from his book. I've decided not to do that. I figured I want you to know *me*, those of you who haven't met me already, and I'd like you to determine then whether my book is worth reading!

You should know about another reason I have in giving these talks. A couple of months ago I made a visit to a psychic I've known for some years now. I write about him in my book. And he said, "Frank, Martha was here for an hour before you came, and she's so excited about your book, and she said she's going to help you write three more books in the next six years." I said, "I don't want to write any more books." He said, "I'm sorry, but there's a lot of light around this, and you're just going to have to do it." Well, these talks I'm giving to you will become the basis for the first of those three books that Martha insists I'm going to write!

Now today I'm going to talk about anger. And I'm going to talk to you about the good news that we have. Now, there's been a lot of bad news that we've had. The economy's crashing, and we have had wars and bitterness and conflict. I'm going to talk about how to have peace in the heart, by healing your anger. That's the good news.

I'm going to illustrate for you the process of changing our minds. You see, we have this capacity to make a choice, a choice between the part of our mind that is basically murderous and hateful, and fearful and guilty; and the part of our mind that knows what compassion and forgiveness are.

I'm going to list eight psychological truths that I believe are true about anger. I'm going to then lay out a metaphysical basis for those ideas. And then I'm going to tell two true stories, one from the East and one from the West, that illustrate how a mind can be healed from fear and guilt and anger, through the power of Love, and thus become open to compassion. Then I'll lay out some factors that seem congruent to both stories, factors we need to look at in order to heal our minds from the anger and move them toward peace, that is to say, what the Course calls "obtaining the Miracle." Then I'm going to throw open the meeting to your discussion and questions. And finally, I'll close with a brief meditation, by reading from the Course what I believe are some very lovely lines.

I see this gathering as a "love fest," because what I experienced when I spoke at another book-signing some time ago there was a palpable sense of love in the air. I hope that that sense will be here for us today.[1] It depends on what you bring to me, and what I bring to you. As Jesus puts it in the Course, "When two are joined in a common goal, Love is present." Our common goal here is to understand how, together, we can heal our anger.

---

[1]   And with those of you who are reading this book!

Chapter 2

Eight Psychological Truths about Anger

So let me start by describing eight facts about anger. I do not expect you to believe me. In fact, I tell my patients, "Don't believe anything I say! I ask only that you think about it. Use your head. See if it fits. If it doesn't fit, throw it out. If it does fit, adopt it, try it out. Experiment and see whether it works." I expect you will have some questions about the ideas I'm going to share with you. Some of them are radical. Others will strike you right off the bat as very logical.

The first fact about anger is this: *Anger kills.* It kills joy; it kills happiness. It also kills bodies. Anger contributes to heart attacks and high blood pressure. I think my dad died of anger. He was a very angry man, and he suffered a massive heart attack at age fifty-five—passed away just like that.

And one of the reasons I believe anger is what killed my dad is this: when I was studying psychoanalysis in Manhattan back in the 1950s, I trained with an analyst who'd had a very interesting job in World War II. He'd been an army psychiatrist, and he'd traveled with a number of other psychiatrists, as part of a government study, to visit all the U.S. Air Corps installations (training centers, airbases, etc.). His job was to observe all the airmen at work, and if he spotted an angry airman, he pulled him immediately off the line (whatever his rank, and that must have gotten this man in trouble with some angry generals because he was only a lieutenant!). Anyway, he took any angry airman he saw off the line, took him to the nearest clinic, and took a sample of his blood. He would then put the man in a quiet, comfortable room, with soft classical music playing, until the guy cooled down. Then he would take a second blood sample, so that he ended up with two samples: a sample of "angry blood" and a sample of what I'll call "less angry blood" (I'm not going to say "loving blood," just "less angry"). Then he would go out and pull another angry airman off the line and get two blood samples from him too, in the same fashion, and this went on for thousands and thousands of instances. And when they analyzed the blood samples, do you know what they found? The "angry blood" had the highest amount of lipids—of cholesterol and triglycerides, which, as you know, are killers. The "less angry blood" had a lower amount of lipids—triglycerides and cholesterol. Anger kills.

And it doesn't just kill the one who's angry. A few months ago, in Kansas I believe, a man was ushering for his church on a Sunday morning, handing out church bulletins, and a guy walked in and blew him away. It turns out the murdered man was a doctor who ran an abortion clinic, and the guy that killed him was so angry about that that he committed murder. And anger killed a security guard at the Holocaust Museum in Washington recently, shot by an eighty-eight-year-old man who was angry at the Jews. Anger kills.

It kills in war too. As an infantry lieutenant in World War II, it was my responsibility to teach eighteen-year-old boys how to kill (I was only eighteen myself!). I was taught how to do that. I was taught, when lunging with a bayonet toward the entrails of the enemy, to scream like a lion and twist the bayonet to eviscerate the internal organs. You know what? I got a feeling eventually of liking that! And it scared me that I could be so pleased, so full of glee to be causing pain and anguish to an enemy. That made me think, "What is this nice young Christian boy doing, having such awful thoughts?" That was partly the reason I decided later to study the mind and try to get rid of that murderous hate, because I knew the guilt I had was so intense.

You see, guilt's what happens when we have the anger. When a boat moves through the water, it leaves behind a track of turbulence, known as the wake. Likewise, when rage flows through the mind, it leaves an instant wake of guilt, guilt that is often repressed and therefore unconscious. And that guilt is hurtful to us.

Let me give one more example of the killing nature of anger, something that on the face of it may seem less dramatic than the anger that generates heart attacks and murder and war. When I was a kid in Scranton, I had a buddy with whom I and some of the other neighborhood boys would play baseball after school. His name was Josie, and he was all-important to us for the simple fact that it was Josie who owned the ball and bat we played with. So we needed Josie! And every evening we'd play until six o'clock. The reason we had to stop at six was because the Catholic church up the street would ring its bell at that hour to signal the start of evening Mass. And at the sound of that bell, Josie would groan, "Jesus Christ, my mother's gonna kill me!" You see, Josie's family was Catholic, and they never missed Mass. And sure enough, instantly we would hear Josie's mother calling, "Josie! Josie!" And Josie would say, "She'll kill me, I tell you!" and then he'd grab his ball and bat and run like hell for home. That was the end of the game, of course. Now, we all knew that Josie would come back to play with us the next afternoon, because his mother never actually killed him! But what Josie knew is what all of us kids knew: that a parent's anger, in a child's mind, is interpreted as death. We deny that. Jesus knew it. In the Sermon on the Mount he said, "You have heard that it was said to the men of old, 'You shall not kill;' and that whoever kills shall be liable to judgment. But I say to you that every one who is angry with his brother shall be liable to judgment" (Matt. 5:21-22).[2] The Course's idea is equally radical: it's either love, or it's murder. Anger kills.

The second fact about anger is this: *all anger is caused by fear.* And when we are fearful, we are fearful for our *bodies.* For example, when I was in the army, I was the leader of a platoon of new recruits, and it was my job to train them. And there was one guy from West Virginia—I remember him well—who was very angry and difficult, because I was the officer and he was the private, and he hated me for it (we were both teenagers, by the way). He hated authority. One day we were doing an exercise, practicing going on patrol, with live ammunition. And at one point he stumbled and said "shit". Well, because we were learning about being on patrol, we were supposed to be absolutely silent. And since I knew that some colonels, my superiors, were watching us, I gave him a severe look and said *shhh!* Well, he had his finger on the trigger of his gun, loaded with live shells, and he turned toward me, and suddenly I was staring into the bore of a 30-caliber rifle. It looked (*makes a large circle with his hands*) about this big. I knew he hated me. And my stomach went *fffwhew;* you know how the stomach goes when you experience the terror of bodily harm—tension in the stomach, tension in the muscles. Luckily he didn't pull the trigger, and when he turned away from me, my fear turned immediately into anger.

---

[2] Some ancient texts add the words "without just cause" to Jesus' statement, so that it reads "everyone who is angry with his brother *without just cause* is liable to judgment." I believe those words were inserted by some ancient editor in an attempt to justify the editor's own anger. All of us want to believe that our anger is just and deserved, and that there is such a thing as righteous anger. Yet in the Course, Jesus states that anger is *never* justified; although, as we shall see, it is *always* forgiven.

I was angry at him because I was so frightened, frightened of my body being blown away.

Here's another example. I had a patient some years back, a patient with some significant psychological problems. I'd been working with him for about four years until one day he came in and said, "Well, I put the gun away that I've been carrying when I came to your office." I said, "What gun?" and he said, "The gun I had." I said, "I hope it wasn't loaded," and he said, "Oh no, it was loaded all right. And I had the safety off, too." Shocked, I said, "Why did you do that?" and he said, "Well, there were those red rays coming out of your eyes, and I was frightened that those red rays might hurt me. So I had that gun ready just in case." My stomach went south at that thought. Then I became very angry at him, from the fear in my gut of my body being blown away. But I quickly recovered and said to myself, "My god, I'm hating my own patient. I've got to make a correction." Which I made, fortunately.

The fear I'm talking about doesn't just arise when our physical bodies are attacked. The same reaction occurs when there's an attack on the *psychological* body. We all have psychological bodies. When one is humiliated, belittled, or confronted with contempt and hatred, one can have the same feeling in the gut, the same tension in the muscles, the same feeling of fear, followed by anger.

The third truth about anger is this: *all anger is a cry for love.* Always a cry for love. When somebody is angry at you, one of the best ways to be at peace is to see their anger as a desperate cry for love, because if they were in that state of love, they would be at peace. And they're yearning for that peace, that love, or they would not be attacking. As one rabbi put it two thousand years back, "Perfect love casts out fear." Another way he could have put that would be, "Fear creates a cloud that masks any awareness of perfect love." Wise man, this Jesus. It's His words we're reading, I believe, when we read *A Course in Miracles.*

You see, there are only two types of data we get from our brothers and sisters in this world. One is love and the other is a cry for love. That's because love is the only thing that's real! And it's so interesting how a true expression of love has the power to touch and bring forth as a response the love that is in us. When I stood in St. Peter's Basilica in Rome and saw Michelangelo's beautiful statue of the *Pieta* in that snow-white marble—such a beautiful expression of the love of a mother for her dead son—well, my heart went out to both the mother and the son, to mothers and sons everywhere, as a matter of fact. Or when you see a mother nursing her baby, and you see her gentle caring for that baby, your heart goes out, because you are seeing the love in that experience. I'm reading a book now called *Three Cups of Tea,* which is the true story of an American mountain climber who, in the process of descending from a failed attempt to reach the summit of K2, got separated from the rest of his climbing party and ended up wandering into a remote area of northern Pakistan, without any food or water. Finally, half-dead, he stumbled into an impoverished Pakistani village where the people took him in and nursed him back to health. These people had nothing, but they fed and clothed him; they killed the fatted calf for him, a stranger. And this man's response was to fall in love with these people and to resolve to do something for them, out of the fullness of this love. So he raised money to build a school for the children of the village, because they had none. We see this kind of love and compassion occasionally in the world. More often, however, we see the opposite. We see schools destroyed in Pakistan and Afghanistan by fundamentalist groups opposed to the education of girls. We see hate, violence, and cruelty. The media is filled with the images and sounds of hate and anger. That's usually the picture the world presents us with: brothers and sisters who are not remembering the love that is in them and who are simultaneously crying out for it.

The fourth characteristic and truth about anger is this: *all anger begins in the mind of the attacker.* When somebody is angry at you,

you have not caused his anger. In fact, his anger has nothing to do with you, even if you have treated him badly. Now, this is a difficult idea. For instance—and let me be very concrete—let's suppose temporarily I lose my mind, at this moment. And I come down there and I start beating at you, shouting "You bitch!" and other awful things. Well, if you become angry at me, *I* have not caused that anger. You see, you have a choice, a choice as to how you will interpret my attack upon you. We forget that, especially under the assault of the moment of anger. It's my anger at *me* that is the problem. *My* fear, *my* insanity. You haven't done anything! However, if you get angry at me—and certainly I *have* been abusing you, and you have a right to do what you can to stop my abuse, a right to call the cops and have me locked up—but you do not have the right to be angry at me. Anger is never justified! (*T-30. VI. 1:1*)[3] Now that's a statement you may have some trouble with. Because we all want to believe our anger is justified. We all want to believe we're unfairly treated. The truth is that all anger is a cry of pain, and that it begins in the mind of the attacker and has *nothing* to do with you. That's not what the world teaches. Remember, folks, I'm posing a radical view from a radical spiritual path.

The fifth truth about anger is this: *we're afraid to express our anger, because we fear the consequences should we let our anger hang out.* We repress our anger, most of the time, because we are afraid that others will reject us as this unpleasant, angry person that nobody wants to have around, and that if we were openly

---

[3] This is the standard annotation referencing *A Course in Miracles*. The Course consists of a Text, a Workbook, and a Manual for Teachers. In the annotation above, *T* stands for Text, *30* is the chapter number, *VI* is the section within the chapter, *1* is the paragraph number of that section, and the final *1* is the sentence number within the paragraph.

expressing our anger, no one would have anything to do with us. So what do we do with our anger? We repress it.

Now, repressing our anger leads to one of two different responses. One, we become depressed. I would say that the world is largely in a state of low-grade depression. As Thoreau said, we live lives of quiet desperation. Most of us are lacking joy, because we are all trying to sit on this anger we have that we are so frightened of expressing. I remember there was a fad in psychotherapy thirty or forty years ago of letting all your anger hang out and then you would feel better. Well, you do temporarily, because you're not repressing your anger, but it doesn't solve the problem. The generator of the anger keeps pumping out rage, and then if you turn into this angry curmudgeon who nobody wants to have around, you have to pay the price of loneliness and isolation, and who wants that? If you have repressed anger, it's like a pressure cooker on the stove: the fear is the fire, the boiling water is the rage, and the sealed lid on the top creates the feeling of depression because we're all steamed up and there's no way to ease the pressure. You can take off the lid, but unless you turn off the fire below, which is fear, you will have a continuous state of depression. That's why, in my practice, what I do is help the patient get free of the fear that is generating the rage. Then there's no need to repress it. The depression is lifted, in direct ratio to the amount of fear and anger that is undone through the work of forgiveness.

The second characteristic that follows from that repression is that *what we repress we project out onto somebody else.* And this particular characteristic is a very important one for us to be aware of. For example—what I hate in me, I see in you, and I dump my guilt for what I hate in me onto you. I say, "You're the bad guy, not me!" The evildoers are always "out there." In recent years, we've had a president who told us just that, that the evildoers are "out there"; that we Americans are a virtuous, wonderful, democratic, peace-loving people; and that we are not the evildoers; *they* are the evildoers. Well, the evildoer (*points to his heart*) is in us! But you see, it makes me feel better (at least temporarily) when I can say, "I'm not as bad as you." We all do that. Individuals as well as nations, we are all the same. And when we project onto others what we have repressed in ourselves, what we're trying to do is alleviate the awful feeling of guilt. And if you can begin to see in yourself this process of projecting your guilt outward—"I'm not bad; somebody else is bad"—well, that is a very important thing to see! A recent example is the former governor of New York, Elliot Spitzer. As attorney general, and as governor too, he was on a crusade to shut down the prostitution trade in New York State. Well, why was he so zealous in attacking the prostitutes? Most likely because of his guilt over his own secret practice of consorting with prostitutes—while at the very same time he was publicly condemning them! It's called projection. Try to see that in yourself, that what you're hating in somebody else is basically what you're hating in you. And then you can take the next step, which I'll describe in more detail later, which is to bring your guilt back to the Love of God for forgiveness, for undoing. Or let me say instead, "Bring it back to the *Love* in you," whether you believe in God or not. Belief in God is an oxymoron anyway. It's not belief in God that puts us in touch with Love. The guys who piloted those planes into the Twin Towers in New York City and killed all those people, and themselves—they believed in God! So it's not belief in God. It's the *experience* of God. The experience of love, not the belief in love. That's the message that I hope to underscore this evening.

The sixth truth about anger is this: *it is a desperate attempt to change behavior in somebody "out there."* When a parent has a child who's not acting the way he wants him to, by getting angry at him the parent hopes to frighten the child enough to make him stop doing what he's doing. How many of you had that kind of a parent? What, nobody? (*Several people raise their hands*) That's more like it! When I was a kid, and I'd sit on the toilet in our apartment—there was only one bathroom—I would stare with a mixture of terror and fascination at my dad's razor strap. Any of you people remember razor straps? Well, my dad sharpened his razor on it, but he also had it there for my rear end when I wasn't doing what he thought I should do![4]

Now, the razor strap story is an example of an attempt to change behavior with an open threat, through a father's wrath expressed in the form of a beating. There's another way parents manipulate behavior in their children, and that's through martyrdom. The martyr, who sighs with deep pain, "Oh, how you've hurt me, my child, by acting the way you have!" The purpose is to create guilt in the child so that his behavior will change to something that suits the martyr better. The martyr's method may be more subtle, but it is no less hateful than the razor strap approach. In the presence of the martyr, the child feels, "Oh my god, what did I do?" I can remember as a five-year-old sitting at dinner with my parents—my folks generally ate in a kind of frosty silence, and you could cut the tension in the air with a knife—and I would think in my child's mind, "What did I do? Did I spill my milk? Did I wet my pants? What?" I thought it was me. Guilt! I remember a cartoon in the *New Yorker* magazine, probably fifty years ago. I liked it so much I cut it out. It showed a little boy sitting on the floor, looking very dejected and depressed and alone. And in the bubble—the cartoon bubble that shows what the little boy is thinking—there's the image of the globe of the earth. And there's a big can of black paint above the earth that's pouring black paint all over it, and that image is the sad thought this sad little boy is having. And the caption underneath the cartoon—obviously spoken by some adult nearby, clearly a parent—reads, "*Now* look what you've done!" That's manipulation through guilt! And it's not just parents who use that strategy. We all do it, in the subtle ways we attempt

---

[4]   It's axiomatic (in the Course's view) that all fear leads eventually, and inevitably, to guilt.

to manipulate spouses or friends by trying to make them feel guilty for their (as we perceive it) shoddy or inappropriate treatment of us.

Let me tell you a story from my own life, from fifty-two years back. It's a story I'm not proud of, but it illustrates my point about anger as a desperate attempt to change someone else's behavior. Martha and I were young then, and we'd recently moved to Manhattan, where I had begun my training as a student of psychoanalysis. We'd rented a small ground floor apartment off Riverside Drive. Now, the living room of this apartment had a row of windows that looked out on the street, but because the apartment was actually below the street level, when you looked out these windows what you saw were the legs of the people walking by on the sidewalk. There were bars on these windows. It was July and very hot, and we had no air conditioner in our apartment because we had no money. It must have been close to one hundred degrees that day, so we'd left all the windows wide open, hoping to catch a cool breeze coming over the Hudson River from New Jersey. So I'm sitting there next to the windows listening to soft music, when suddenly I hear "Bang! Bang! Bang! Bang! Bang! Bang! Bang!" So I look out the windows, and I see this little child's legs. The kid obviously has a stick, and he's running by and hitting the stick against these bars that were placed there to protect from people breaking into the apartment. So I call out the window, "Please, don't do that!" And for an answer I get "Bang! Bang! Bang! Bang! Bang! Bang! Bang!" So I say, a little louder this time, "Please stop that!" And again, "Bang! Bang! Bang! Bang! Bang! Bang! Bang!" My god, what was happening? I became furious! I now understand that in that moment I was fearing my own helplessness, and—thinking in my desperation that anger could change behavior—I ran out of that apartment in a towering rage. There on the sidewalk was the little boy with the stick. I picked him up and I shook him, shouting, "Didn't you hear me screaming at you?" I really was so angry I could have killed him. Well, his parents were standing about forty feet away, talking to the doorman, and the mother cries out, "Call the police!" Then the father comes running over, shouting—and I'll never forget this—"He's deaf, for God's sake! He's deaf!" And the father snatches the kid, terrified and crying, away from me. Now the guilt hits me. God, I felt (*gestures*) that big! Well, the police came, and I really had to do a song and dance to talk them out of arresting me. Fortunately, they let me off with a stern warning that if I ever got caught coming after a defenseless child like that again, I'd be doing time. And I thought to myself, "Oh, I've got to do something with this rage." I learned a lesson that day: Get to work on that anger! It's cruel to the kid, and it's cruel to me. An attempt to change behavior of something out there . . .

The seventh truth about anger is this: *all anger starts with a belief in separation.* I'm angry at you because you're not like me. For instance, if you're a liberal Democrat, and you see a conservative Republican like Rush Limbaugh, you hate him because he's not like you. That's separation. (There are many forms; the Rush Limbaugh example just happens to be the one that comes to my mind! [*laughter*] I guess you can spot my political beliefs right off the bat.) Anyway, anger perpetuates and keeps separation going. For example, I know people who hold onto and cherish their anger as something that defines their personal style, something that makes them special. On the other extreme are people who always try to be piously sweet and nice because they want to be seen as especially loving, in other words, different from, and better than, you and me. It's still the same thing: separation.

We're separated by form. I'm an old man with male organs, and here in the front row is a young woman with female organs. Quite a difference! But that's a difference in form only. Behind the body, and behind the personality, there is the essence of the One Mind. There is a "right mind" and a "wrong mind" according to the Course's view, which I will articulate shortly, because the Course shows us a way to heal, or undo, that part of the mind it calls the "wrong mind," the fearful, guilty, hateful part. The Course in its holiness, its blessedness, is offering us a gift when it says to us, "There is another way." Another way to perceive ourselves and another way to perceive the world. That's the good news. And let me remind you that the purpose of my talking to you today is to bring good news!

The eighth and final truth about anger is this: *the only person hurt by anger is the one who is angry.* Now you may ask about that little boy I picked up and shook in my hate fifty-two years ago—was he hurt? You bet his personality was hurt! Why, he may be on some shrink's couch this very moment complaining about the horrible childhood trauma he suffered when some strange man attacked him out of the blue, and how that trauma has been messing up his life ever since! And yes, I could have hurt that kid's body if I'd pounded him into the wall, which is what I wanted to do in that moment of murderous hate. But that kid is not his personality, and he's not his body. He is (and this is the good news of *A Course in Miracles*) nothing less than the holiness of the love of God that lives, eternally, in his own mind. You may not believe that, but please remember that I asked you not to believe anything I say! Just think about it.

So the only person hurt by anger is the one who is angry. You see, when you're angry, you're miserable; you're in deep anguish. And you're guilty! It's impossible to be angry without being guilty. And guilt is the major problem we have. When we are guilty, we make misery in the world in order to punish ourselves, because we think we deserve punishment. We think we don't deserve good things, or anything that is of love, or God, because we're convinced we're so bad, so sinful. But that's an illusion, brothers and sisters, as we're going to find out.

Chapter 3

The Geography of the Mind

To help you better understand how the mind works, I'm going to describe for you (in metaphorical terms) its structure (*draws an illustration on a whiteboard*). (*See page 34.*)

This is our mind—my mind and your mind, everybody's mind. By the way, I have four children, and all of them are artists. And you can see from the quality of my drawing that they did not inherit their artistic skills from me! No, they got those genes from Martha. Now, you'll remember that, in the Course's view, the mind is seemingly split—split into what we'll call the right mind, up here; and down below, the wrong mind, also known as the ego. Let's look at the ego first.

In the ego we find body-based fear. We find fear and attack and blame. This is the part of the mind that is always "down on us." It judges us for our errors. It feels that we're never good enough. It's convinced that we can't do anything right. Am I talking in a way that anybody can identify with? (*Most in the audience raise their hands.*) Oh, I'm glad. I don't mean I'm glad that you have fear and judgment in your mind—No, I'm glad you understand what I'm talking about! Because what I'm telling you isn't easy to accept.

The ego wants power, wants to control the world because it's frightened. And nobody wants control who isn't frightened.

34

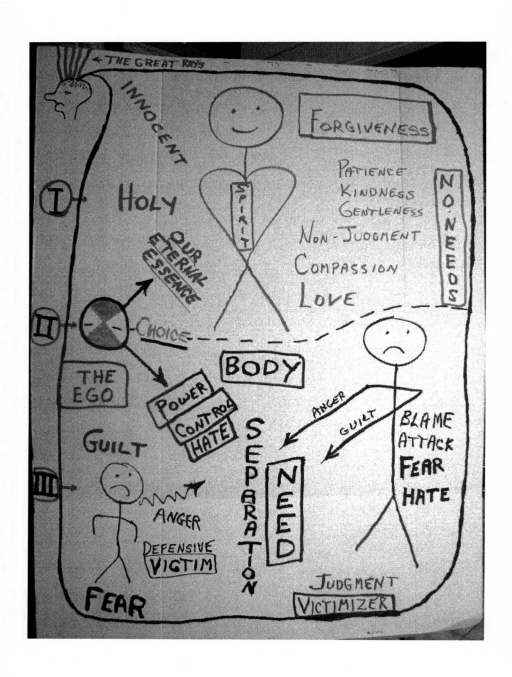

The ego is full of hate. At the bottom of the ego's thought structure is the wish to kill. And every time we have a murderous thought—which is much more often than we'd like to admit!—there is guilt. That's the deeper meaning, to me, of the *New Yorker* cartoon of the little boy: "*Now* look what you've done!" You see, the little boy believes, as we all believe, that what we are in the secret core of our being is a killer. This is the self-image, usually unconscious, of the warring, hateful, guilty part of the mind that the Course calls the ego. Yet the ego is not real! It's something we make up, out of whole cloth. It feels real. It feels very real. You feel it in the sinking feeling in your gut, you feel it in your hateful fury, you feel it in your guilt, and you feel it in your terror.

There is a *victimizer* in this part of the mind, and there is a *victim* that is defensive and fearful of judgment. We love being a victim! We all love it, and it's very hard for us to get that. But as my mentor Ken Wapnick puts it, the ego is like some little beady-eyed creature looking at you over a wall and waiting, just waiting, for somebody to cut you off on the highway, or somebody to disappoint you or let you down, or when you call up to try to get your computer fixed and some person in India isn't able to help you and you fly into a rage—because really, in your secret ego heart, you're glad that they caused you misery! Because now you can blame somebody else. It's *they* who are bad, not me.

And the truth is that we, you and I, live here (in the ego mind) 24/7. Our nightmares come from here. And the nightmares we make in our waking life come from here. For instance, I saw a patient today who came in very upset. What had happened was that earlier in the day she'd had a very happy time playing with her young child. She then (in a flash, and just below the level of consciousness) became guilty in her mind about all this happiness she was experiencing with her child. I mean, who was *she* to be deserving of all that happiness? So the next thing she does is getting a little too rambunctious in her play, and the child accidentally pokes her in the eye, at which point she shoves the child, and the child falls and hurts himself. So now here is my patient coming to me feeling guilty about being a terrible mother who hurts her child. Well, folks, she set it all up. Unconsciously and in the twinkling of an eye, but she set it up. She sabotaged her own happiness, because she was so frightened of the love that she had been experiencing with her child. Yes, frightened of the love. That's another thought. There's a quote in the Course that says, "You think you fear your hate. You do not fear your hate as much as you fear love." That's so weird! "What do you mean," you say, "that I fear love? I *want* love. I like how it feels." But there's another part of your mind that says, "No way." The Course puts it like this: "When the light (which is love) draws near, you rush to darkness; sometimes to lesser forms of fear, and sometimes to stark terror." (*T-18.III.2:1-2*)

Here's a further illustration. Recently, I had lunch at a restaurant with a friend of mine who'd just read my book. He told me how there were things in my book that really spoke to him, really touched his heart. And we were very close to each other at that moment, closer than we'd ever been. And I leave the restaurant and get in my car; always when I get in my car, I look in all three mirrors before I back up, and then I back up slowly. But after having had that experience with my friend, I don't look back, and I don't check my mirrors; I hit the accelerator, and back smack into a truck behind me. It cost me a thousand bucks to fix my car. Fortunately, there was a steel bumper on the truck I hit, so I didn't cause any damage there. And thank God that there was no human being walking behind me! If it had been an accident where the cops had been called, they would have said, "You're an eighty-three-year-old man? I don't know whether you should be driving a car at all." So I was happy that I didn't lose my license! But that incident was an illustration of my fear of love, for certainly I had to have been disoriented by fear to have been so uncharacteristically careless in backing up my car. And it must have been the experience I'd just had with my friend, the experience of joining and sharing and love, that caused me to panic. Observe how often that is. Sometimes,

I would embrace Martha and feel such love. And then I would notice a mole on her neck. And I'd say to myself, "Why does she have that mole?" And the love was gone just like that! That's what we do in our insanity, my friends. It sounds crazy, right? And that's the Course's view, that the world is insane. This is Ward 8, Bellevue, here! This is a loony bin, and we're all loonies because we all live in the ego 99.9 percent of the time.

This (*points to "wrong mind" part of the drawing*) is not what we are, though it seems like we're this. This (*points to "right mind"*) is what we are. Now you don't have to believe in God to know that this is what you are. I said earlier, belief in God is an oxymoron. But all of us are capable of getting to the truth that this part of your mind is indeed the essence of what you are. It has a quality of patience and kindness, of gentleness and non-judgment, compassion and love.

Remember, we're looking at a *seemingly* split mind. That's why I've drawn a broken line where the split *seems* to be. But there is no split! We make up the illusion of all this ego content; then we forget we made it up and start believing it's real. This (*points to the "right mind" part of the drawing*) is what we really are and which the ego obscures. It is holiness. It is eternal love. It is the real me. That deaf little boy I attacked in my rage all those years ago—perhaps, I did wound his self-esteem, and if I'd pounded him into the wall like I'd wanted to, I certainly would have hurt his body. But that little boy is not that. He's not his body or his personality. No, *this* is what he is. I hope he knows that. I hope he's learned it. This brings peace because it's love. It is eternal and unchanging. In the Course it's often referred to as light. And it is eternal, it never dies.

How do I know it never dies? I mentioned that my wife passed away four years ago last Monday. Her body died. *She is not her body.* Her personality died. *She is not her personality.* What was she? She was this holy essence, capable of forgiveness and compassion that was alive in the gentle woman I knew as Martha. In fact, I have a story about that that's in my book. You see, she had dementia her last five years, a form that progressed very rapidly. The third year into that, she wasn't able to towel off her body after a shower. So the morning ritual was like this: I'd help her undress; she'd step in the shower; I'd hand her the shampoo; she'd use the shampoo and hand it back. And when she was through washing, she'd open the door, and I would stand there with the towel and I'd dry her off. I'd start with her hair and work my way down to the rest of her body. And one morning, I got to her hips, and she said, "Frank, I've noticed that you're not attracted to my body anymore." I froze. What was I going to say? I could have lied and said, "Oh, I'm still attracted." But Martha could spot a lie a mile away. So I couldn't say that. So I said, "No, your body is not attractive. It's wasting with the age and dementia. But I remind you, I am attracted to *you*. And you are not your body. I'm attracted to your kindness, your gentleness, your compassion, your capacity to love and forgive." And there was a slight pause and she said, "Oh, I forgot." We all forget. This is what we are. We think we're this (the ego), because we're in this state so often. My wife forgot, I forget, you forget. Well, I'm calling us all to remember tonight.

This is the good news, folks. Because when we begin to see how the ego works in our own mind and come to understand it a little, we can make a correction by forgiving ourselves for our silliness in believing that what the world had taught us is real. So far I've talked about two parts of the mind, one being the ego and the other the Holiness given to us at our creation as our inheritance. But there is a third part to your mind. And this part is able to *choose* between fear and judgment on one side, and love on the other. Ken Wapnick refers to this part of the mind as the decision-maker.

This capacity for choice, I believe, came out of the love of our Creator, which endows us with the freedom to make a choice. You cannot pull apart freedom and love. They go together. And if ever you're questioning whether an action is loving or not, ask whether freedom is involved in it. Freedom for your brother, freedom for yourself. There's a Course quote that I put on the whiteboard in our kitchen several years ago, which helped my marriage very much. Martha said to me one day, "You know, I'm glad you put that quote up there." I was glad she was glad, and this is the quote from the very end of chapter eleven of the Course text: "I give you to the Holy Spirit as part of myself (because we're all one!), and I know you will be released unless I choose to use you to imprison myself. In the name of my freedom I release you; because I know we will be released together." That's the oneness, the forgiveness—the giving up of the exploitation (for our own perceived needs and ends) of others. Mutual exploitation, in the Course's view, is the basis of most of our relationships in the world, what the Course calls "special relationships." We use and exploit others for our egoistic purposes. "Give me the Oreo cookie now, Mom, not later, or I'll throw a tantrum and then you'll feel bad!" That's what special relationships are about: I want what I want when I want it. And someone else is supposed to provide it for us.

That's why the unhappy guy up here in my drawing is so unhappy—because he's listening to his ego. So what then, you may ask, are these rays I've drawn around his head? Well, I've tried there (in my inept way) to illustrate what the Course calls the "Great Rays." The great rays extend from our mind back into the darkness to reach all of your brothers and sisters and finally reaching all the way to heaven. So in reality, we're not separated. You and I and God are all connected by these great rays. It's the great rays that save us from the hell of the ego idea that we are separate.

At least four or five times a day, I pray a prayer taken from lesson 232 of the Course. It goes like this: "Be in my mind, Father, as I wake; and shine on me throughout the day today. Let every minute be a time in which I dwell with You. And let me not forget my hourly thanksgiving that You have remained with me and always will be there to hear my every call to You and answer me. As evening comes, let all my thoughts still be of You and of Your Love. And let me sleep sure of my safety, certain of your care, and happily aware that I am Your Son." I love that. It is a form of joining with the Great Rays. It's the good news I told you about.

Chapter 4

Two Stories—East and West

I'm going to tell you two stories, one about a man from the East and the other about a man from the West, and then I'm going to take your questions. And hopefully, we'll have a little time left over for me to sign your books. By the way, how many of you have books for me to sign? (*An audience member raises her hand.*) Oh, good, just one! [*laughter*] That gives us more time to talk and more time for questions!

First, the story about the man from the East, from Tibet actually. It's a story that impressed me very much, and it appeared in the summer of 1989 in the *Harvard Medical Alumni Bulletin*[5], in an article written by a wonderful guy named Albert Crum, who was a psychiatrist at NYU. Crum had undertaken a study of people that he called "triumphant persons." And one of these triumphant persons he studied, and writes about in his article, is this man from Tibet.

As you know, fifty years ago, China decided to annex Tibet, to erase any vestiges of Tibet as an independent state and to make it

---

5 "Triumph over Torture—Against All Odds," Summer 1989, Vol. 63, No.1.

into a province of China. They destroyed hundreds of monasteries (remember that Tibet was at that time a Buddhist theocracy), and they slaughtered thousands of monks. Their intent was to capture the Dalai Lama. They thought if they could break his spirit, through torture, and get him to recant his Buddhist beliefs and embrace Maoism instead, they could control the people of Tibet more easily. But as you know, the Dalai Lama escaped into India. The Chinese did manage to capture, however, the personal physician to the Dalai Lama, a man by the name of Dr. Tenzin Choedrak.

Dr. Choedrak was thirty-six years old at the time of his capture. He was taken, along with seventy-five other high-echelon monks, to a notorious prison in China. They kept him in solitary confinement for twenty years.[6] And in that solitary confinement he was tortured daily. Now, for some of you who are squeamish about hearing graphic details of torture, please cover your ears, because I'm going to describe some of the torture he experienced.

In one of the forms of torture, the Chinese put ropes around and under his shoulders; they would then suddenly jerk the ropes in such a way that the shoulder joints were pulled and twisted out of their sockets. The jerk and twist was so fast and traumatic that it created a crescendo of pain, like an electric fire racing through Dr. Choedrak's body, producing loss of bladder and bowel control and, finally, unconsciousness. Ligaments and tendons in the shoulders were torn and ruptured irreparably.

The Chinese put chains around Dr. Choedrak's neck, his hands, and his legs so that if he moved his body the chains became tighter. Let me read you what the author of the article writes about this form of torture: "The body gradually becomes numbed; the fluid balance of the body becomes so disturbed by trauma that the thirst for water became unbearable. Such thirst often produces a psychosis."

---

[6] See also *The Rainbow Palace*, Bantam Books, 2000.

He was starved to the point where, in order to get enough protein, he would eat pieces of his leather jacket, until he had eaten the entire jacket. His fecal matter was not removed from his cell. And he would go through his fecal matter in search of maggots, and when he found some, because maggots are protein, he would eat those in order to stay alive.

He was routinely beaten about the head with the heel of a rubber boot, to the point where he was deafened in one ear and blinded in one eye. When he walked into Dr. Crum's office in New York years later, not long after the Chinese finally released him, the secretary called Dr. Crum and said, "What a man! I never met such a calm man in my life." And as he came in, Crum—after first noticing that his head was seriously tilted to one side, and that most of his teeth had been knocked out—was impressed by the serenity and gentleness he met. The handshake was soft, the eyes were clear, the brow was serene, and his voice was gentle. And Crum wondered—and this is why he had asked to meet him—how come a guy who has experienced such prolonged horror, over twenty years of it, doesn't suffer from post traumatic stress syndrome? (You'll recall how so many of our soldiers returning from Iraq and Afghanistan suffer from the intense and chronic anguish of PTSS.) So Crum asked him, "Dr. Choedrak, how come you're so gentle? You don't have any nightmares, and you're not plagued by fears or anguish, or consumed by hatred."

Now, Dr. Choedrak had been raised by monks since the age of ten. His mother had died, his father had remarried, and his grandmother had taken him to a monastery and asked the monks to adopt him and raise him because, as the grandmother told the monks, "His stepmother can't stand him." So he grew up in a monastery. We all should be so lucky! He said to Dr. Crum, "Well, I was taught that your enemy is there to teach you patience," same as *A Course in Miracles,* which tells us that the difficult people in our lives are there to teach us how to love. He said, "I was taught that extreme troubles increase our wisdom. And as a physician of Tibetan medicine, I was taught that a doctor must possess a 'peaceful wind energy,' because the patient comes to him with a 'typhoon energy,' a tumultuous energy, and if the doctor has a wild and tumultuous energy, it will only increase the tumult in his patient." What he was saying was that being at peace is healing to a patient who is panicked and in pain. He said, "I was also taught to respect the dignity of all my brothers. So I respected the dignity of my torturer." He said, "We are taught that violence breeds violence, and love breeds love. So I said to myself, whenever I saw my torturer, 'The potential Buddha is in that torturer, as the potential Buddha is in me. We are the same. Not different, the same.' And when I saw the potential Buddha in my torturer, how could I hate him?" How about that?

He said, "I was taught to look within, at my inner motives, and not to look outside for a solution to my problems." This is the same as the Course and same as Western psychotherapy. And he also said, "I was taught to have a higher purpose." That's like the case of the Austrian-Jewish psychiatrist Dr. Victor Frankel, who attributed his ability to endure Auschwitz with serenity because he knew he had a higher purpose, an inner meaning and value beyond the egotism of the body and the interests of the "small S" self.

And finally, Dr. Choedrak said, "Especially when they put the ropes around my arms, I couldn't meditate or be in any state of peace when that happened. So what I learned to do was to meditate *before* the torture and prepare my mind for the horror that was to come." I like that idea. We could all use that idea. We might learn to prepare our minds so as to be able to remain at peace in anticipation of some stressful event we are about to experience. (I will illustrate this process in my story about the man from the West.)

But then Crum wondered, how come he wasn't killed? After all, seventy-two of the seventy-six Tibetan monks taken to that notorious Chinese prison were killed after they were tortured. How come Choedrak wasn't? Crum's answer was twofold. He realized that if Choedrak had hated his torturer, the torturer would have known it, and the torturer's own hatred would have increased and might have driven him to the point where he would have killed him. The 'typhoon energy' of the torturer, to use Choedrak's own terminology, would have increased and would then have violently destroyed him.

The second reason Crum came up with as to why Choedrak wasn't killed was that he didn't grovel or humiliate himself by begging for mercy, because groveling and begging (Crum knew, as we all do) breed contempt, and more contempt in the mind of his torturer may have driven him to kill. By being in a habitual posture of serenity of mind, Choedrak surely saved his life. Love saves; anger kills. And that's the story of the man from the East.

≈

Now for the story of the man from the West—a man, in fact, from this country. He was a patient of mine for many years, so I will not use his real name. Let's call him Bill.

Now, Bill had two children, a boy and a girl. His daughter seemed, from birth, to be unusually frightened. Everything seemed to frighten her. She bit her nails. She needed constant comforting, which she received from her mother. Her dad, you see, was totally devoted, as many men of his generation were, to his business, to making lots of money to support the family, and he believed the child-rearing was his wife's responsibility. When he started working with me years later, after his children were grown, he admitted to me that he felt regret that he hadn't been more involved with them. "If I had it to do over again," he told me, "I would spend more time with my kids." (I think the current generation of young people has a more enlightened idea about the place of the father in raising children. At least I hope they do.)

Anyway, not only Bill didn't spend time with his kids, but he actually neglected them, through his single-minded focus on his work. But he was also a very frightened man and therefore a very angry man. This made him judgmental, autocratic, and coercive toward his children, which made his daughter even more frightened, for as I mentioned before, a young child interprets the anger of a parent as death. And Bill had no idea how to relate to his daughter, or how to help her with her fear.

Fast forward to twenty years later. His daughter has grown up, graduated from college, and found a job in San Francisco. And one night she goes to visit a friend, a single woman like herself, and when she knocks on the door of this friend's apartment, the door is opened by a strange black man with a knife who grabs her and pulls her into the apartment. Inside is her friend, tied up on the bed. The man ties her up too and pushes her into the bathroom, and there in the bathroom she is able to hear this man raping her friend. The man then comes for her but fortunately doesn't have it in him to perform a second rape. But as he leaves the apartment, he threatens to kill her and her friend if they go to the police.

Well, they do go to the police, the rapist is captured, and it turns out he is a serial rapist who has been victimizing young blonde women in the Mission District for some years. Bill's daughter has to go and identify him in a lineup, which for her is extremely traumatizing. In fact, for many months, she's unable to pass a black man on the street without feeling unbearable panic. And the whole rape experience keeps replaying itself in her mind, both when she's awake and at night in the form of terrible nightmares.

So she asks her parents for money to go to a therapist for treatment, and Bill and his wife, of course, send it to her. Now at that time (the late 1970s) there was a viewpoint among many therapists that if a woman has an unusually severe and traumatizing reaction to a rape experience, then that means she must have had some experience of sexual abuse during her childhood, an experience that has subsequently been repressed and is therefore unconscious. And because Bill had been a distant, severe, and angry father during the early years of his daughter's childhood, the daughter and her therapist concluded that the only person who could possibly have been her sexual abuser was her father.

So as a consequence, his daughter decides she will have nothing to do with Bill. And for the next ten years, there are no letters answered, no telephone calls taken, and no communication whatsoever with her father. It is very painful for the both of them.

Now, during this period in which his daughter is incommunicado, Bill begins his work with me. Over many, many sessions together, we try to come up with any evidence that Bill had indeed sexually abused his daughter. Bill has no memory of having done such a thing. So we look carefully at how denial works—that if one has done something so awful as to have abused his own child sexually, then one would usually automatically repress that fact out of awareness, just as we repress (as I explained earlier) our hate and our guilt so that we can tell ourselves, "It's not me."

But we can't find anything in Bill's case. I even send him to a hypnotist. Finally, the only thing we're able to conclude is that his daughter probably felt a lot of hatred for Bill (because he'd been such an unloving parent)—for which she had to have felt guilt and therefore needed to justify her hatred by choosing to see her father as the "evildoer," in this case, a monster who has sex with his children.

In any event, after ten years of no communication with his daughter, Bill's phone rings one weekend. He picks it up and hears his daughter's voice. She says, "Hi, Dad," and his heart leaps with joy. Then she says, "How about you and Mom coming for a visit?" His heart leaps again, and he answers joyfully (by this point, Bill has learned a great deal about joy through studying the Course with me), "Oh yes, that would be great!" Then she says, "Wait a minute, Dad. It's not over yet." Well, he knows what that means. It means that when he visits, he's going to be confronted with more hate!

So I help him prepare for the visit. He's actually dreading going. So I say to him, "There are certain lessons in the Course that help you deal with hatred and attack." And then I list the lessons that

I want him to meditate on before he sees his daughter. They are as follows:

1. *I could see peace instead of this.* In other words, Bill could choose to see his daughter as healed and whole and possessing the love *behind* the obvious form of her painful attack.
2. *My mind is a part of God's. I am very holy.* Remember the "Great Rays" that I've tried to show in my drawing and how they connect us to love, the spirit of Love that is eternal. Those same rays connect Bill eternally to his daughter, and both of them to the rest of their brothers and sisters and, in essence, to God himself.
3. *My holiness blesses the world.* Bill has the power to see the Christ (the spirit of Love) in his daughter instead of reacting defensively and counterattacking her on the ego level.
4. *There's nothing my holiness cannot do.* Love (that's another word for "holiness") is more powerful than all the hatred and attack in the world.

I remind Bill that if his daughter is attacking him for abusing her, she must be guilty about all the ways in which she has abused herself (In fact, we all have suffered abuse and been abusive in some form during our lifetimes). If Bill can see that, that his daughter's attack is a projection of her own self-hate, then that will indeed help him to "see peace" instead.

And so Bill prepares. He prepares on the plane to California. When the daughter and her husband meet him and her mother at the airport, she doesn't look her father in the eye. She won't hug him. She's completely cool toward him. A real cool cat.

This goes on for about three days. And then she says, "Okay, Dad, it's time for our talk." So Bill knows this was *the* moment when he could "see peace instead of this!"

They excuse their respective spouses. And Bill sits on one end of the couch, and his daughter on the other. And for what seems to him like two hours, he gets hate. He gets attack, attack, attack. *You didn't do this; you didn't do that. How could you treat me so bad? How could you be such a terrible father? My marriage is a failure because of you; I can't have children because of you; I'm a total wreck because of you*—he gets the whole *shpiel*.

And Bill remembers to do what I had suggested, and not become fearful or defensive. There's a Course quote that says, "Defenses make what they defend against," which means that defending yourself simply generates more attack. And yes, defenses are a form of attack! So all during his daughter's tirade, he is silent; he is remembering that not only can he not be hurt by the hatred, but that he can see beyond the hatred. He can see the light of eternal Love shining in his daughter, even as it shines in his own mind—the light that is not lessened by the ego, but only obscured; the light that is the same as it has always been since its birth in eternity.

And finally after much haranguing, Bill's daughter says to him, "Damn it, Dad! What bothers me most is that you aren't saying 'Mea culpa!' You're not crying with me and beating your breast and admitting how awful you've been!" And he replies, "Well, I've told you before, and I'll tell you again. I was not an adequate father to you. I know I've been an abusive father, in terms of my anger and my distance and my inability to love. I didn't know about love then. I knew about anger, and I knew about fear. But since that time I've learned a little something about love, and I have that little bit of love now to offer you, if you want it. It's available."

And then Bill notices (as he told me later) that the narrow slits of hateful eyes open a little bit, and he sees coming from the dark eyes a tiny spark. He sees the brow that was furrowed a little less furrowed and the tight lips and jaw eased a bit and softened, and he thinks maybe it's a miracle.

And a miracle is what it is, because in the week that follows his daughter gives him a tentative hug now and then, hugs that become warmer as the days go on. She begins to suggest beautiful local spots that Bill and his wife can visit, and, before they leave for home, she accompanies them on some of these visits.

And over the years since then, Bill begins to get e-mails from his daughter with Xs and Os at the end of them, and just recently, an e-mail that ends, "Dad, I'm so glad you're my dad! I love you."

The Course defines the miracle as that holy instant "When an ancient hate is changed to a current love." That's what happened with Bill and his daughter. And that's my story from the West.

≈

Before I take your questions, I'd like to summarize this process, which is often a very long process, of healing your mind of its anger. First, it's important to become aware of the murderous hate that you have in your mind, and not deny it. Second, you must begin to see all the pain and anguish that that hateful anger brings you, and the very real life consequences it leads to, and which are so hurtful to you. Third, this awareness must lead you to the point where you say, "I don't want it. I don't want the pain anymore." Fourth, you begin to discern the fact that you have another choice, that you don't have to stay in this hell of defensiveness and self-hate. You can return to the awareness of Love's presence in your mind by taking your dark thoughts, your hatred, and your anger, to the forgiveness that is your inheritance.

And finally, what's important in terms of the process of healing is that, even if you don't choose the peace, you're forgiven! You're forgiven if you *don't* heal the ego. It's not a matter of outcome. So if you are anguished and the ego is screaming and you have not gained the peace, well, brothers and sisters, you are *still* forgiven. You are just not quite yet remembering (as Martha didn't remember after her shower that day). We don't remember. But if you remember, you're at peace. And the good news is that, sooner or later, we will *all* remember. It's a done deal!

Chapter 5

Questions and Answers

I'm now ready for your questions. By the way, I have only half an ear—the rest I left in Germany in World War II! So I ask that you please speak up.

Q. In our contemporary global world, isn't there justifiable and right and ethical and moral anger? If we have this anger, won't we try to organize and change the corruption and the meanness and the injustice of the world? Aren't these all things we should be angry about?

A. Wonderful question. This woman is a lovely woman because she cares about the world we live in. Did you hear her question in the back? You did? My god, your ears are better than mine, and I was right up close! Her question deals with her awareness of the horrible ways in which the world is being abused: global warming is being discounted; we're not attending correctly to the healing of our planet with sufficient speed or urgency; and—she didn't say this, but I'm adding it anyway—it may be that we will destroy the world. (*To the questioner*) Have I gotten the gist of your question right? (*The questioner nods*) And you're very angry about these things, correct?

Q. Yes, I'm very angry.

A. If you were in my office, I'd work with your anger. I'm not going to do that now, but I will take a posture. Let me try to restate your feeling: *"If I weren't so angry, I wouldn't be doing anything about the injustices in the world. And I'm glad I'm angry because it activates me to make some change."* Do I have that right? (*The questioner nods*) Well, that's a false idea. The fallacy in that is that it assumes that only anger motivates us. Now it does motivate us. I know that. I used to be, back in the 1960s, what they called a "peacenik." I marched on to the Pentagon. I shouted, "LBJ, how many children have you killed today?" I was a pacifist who was furiously, viciously angry. Now that's an oxymoron for you! I did the so-called peace marches with other angry people around me, and I finally got to the point where I said to myself, "Somehow this doesn't add up. Something's wrong with this picture! I'm not peaceful. I'm hating!" So I'm saying to you that it's possible, out of your *love* for the planet, to do actively what you can to heal it, in any way you can, including your votes for your congressmen, or through your contributions to groups like the Sierra Club or other environmental organizations, which I mention because I'm a contributor to those particular forms. I share your values about the world. But you don't need to be angry in order to act in a way that is helpful. The disadvantage of your position is that your body is paying a price for the angry experience you are having. I invite you to turn instead to your love for your motivation, because you'll be more peaceful and happier, and you will live longer. And I would wish you a long life. (*Applause*) Does someone else have a question?

Q. *If you can't use anger or punishment or manipulation or martyrdom, how do you parent?* (*laughter*)

A. You have children?

Q. *Not yet. My husband and I are trying. We have a dog, though.* (*Laughter*)

A. That's good practice! (*Laughter*) Well, I'll tell you what I've learned. I was not an adequate parent. At the time I was raising my children, I didn't know about love. But I've learned this much: if you can see your child as equal to you, even though you as the parent are wiser and more experienced, well then, you are on the right track. This does not mean you relinquish your responsibility for the behavior of your child. In fact, I urge you to have very strict expectations of your child. You're the boss. It's up to you to train them. One way you can love your child is to take the authority of being the parent. I believe that one of the weaknesses in the current philosophy of parenting is that the child runs the family! And that generates hatred in the child because he cannot respect his parents. The parents are not acting respectably. The job of the parent is to be in control of the child and to teach him how to live in the world. And you can be properly authoritative without being an authoritarian; the first is based on love, the other on fear.

The second thing about parenting is healing your mind of your guilt and your fear and your hate—your *murderous* hate, and I know you have murderous hate . . . (*Laughter*) We all do! We're all murderers! We're all thieves. We're all pimps and prostitutes. That's the ego mind, folks, (*points to the drawing*) down here. But that is not us. *This*, up here, is us. Heal your mind by choosing forgiveness for yourself, and you become for your child a living testimony of love. And you will know what to do, when to do it, what to say, and what not to. You will know all this when you become aware that there is a part of your mind that loves you and knows what's best for you.

I repeat again: see that child as the same as you, as equal to you, though *not* equal. Let's say your child is acting "bad," and you get mad at that child. At the moment that you're mad, don't judge being mad. Because the minute you judge it, you're going to repress it, and you're going to create more trouble, including guilt. What's important to do at that particular moment is to forgive yourself for listening to the wrong side of your mind and to pray mightily for help in seeing you are forgiven for making a mistake. Pray to whomever you pray, even if that be only the part of your mind you see as loving. That's really where the prayer goes anyway—from you *to* you. Pray to see that, if you are angry at that child for, say, his stubbornness, then you are hating you for your own stubbornness. You're hating the child in you that is capable of the exact same behavior. Just ask your own parents. They'll tell you! Have I answered your question?

Q. Yes.

A. It's not about using talk or words with your child either. It's your *experience*. You teach out of your authentic experience of what you are. I finally learned that. I used to think you could preach and get across the message that way. But that's not true, because you can't! Another question . . .

Q. *Given your drawing up there, it seems that we spend a lot of time in the bottom half of the picture.*

A. We sure do. So what's the problem?

Q. *How do we get out?*

A. The problem is that you're not laughing at it! That's the problem. I love the line in the Course where Jesus says the world will end in laughter. You laugh in the end because you finally see the silliness of all this; you finally understand that this is a loony bin and we are the loonies. And none of it is real! So now at last you can smile and laugh at how silly you've been to believe in all these mistaken ideas that have given you so much misery. All you have to do is to look at it and see there's nothing to feel guilty about. See it with Jesus holding your hand—or Elijah or Mohammed or Buddha, it doesn't matter. But I do that all the time. I say, "Gentle Jesus, hold my hand and help me see I am forgiven for my mistaken thought."

Let me illustrate with a story I tell in my book. During the last year of Martha's life I could no longer sleep in the same bed with her because in her dementia she tossed and turned constantly all night long. So I slept in a room about thirty feet away. One night I had gotten her dressed for bed. She had to wear a diaper at this point because she was incontinent. I helped her with that, put her into bed, and went back to the other room to sleep, hoping that everything would be nice for the night.

Well, it wasn't nice. It turned out to be a living nightmare, in fact, because shortly after climbing into my bed, I heard a loud thump coming from Martha's room. My bed actually shook for a moment. And I thought, "Oh my god, she's fallen. She's gotten out of bed and fallen." She had osteoporosis, so I thought, "She's broken her hip or some other bone."

I found her crumpled on the floor of her bedroom. She said, "I think I fell." I said, "I think you fell, too. Let me help you." And as I lifted her up from the floor, she screamed. It was a cry of pain such as I'd never heard in the fifty-two years I'd been married to her. In fact, she had never screamed. It tore my heart out. But fortunately, when I had her erect, she seemed okay. I walked her over to the bed. But as I lay her down, she screamed again. I thought, "My god, I don't know how much I can take of that scream." It pierced my heart. I said to her, "Maybe we should call 911." And she said, typically, "No no, I'll be fine in the morning. Maybe some Tylenol will help."

So I gave her some Tylenol, but I'm thinking, "For that scream I don't think Tylenol's going to cut the mustard." Then I went back to my room, hoping that now we can sleep.

Sorry. Less than two hours later, I hear her calling from her room, "Frank, help me go to the bathroom." So I walk to her bedroom, and as I lift her out of her bed, she screams again. I help her to the bathroom, remove her diaper, help her get on the toilet, re-diaper her when she's finished, and take her back to her bed. But as I lay her down, there's the scream again.

Now this happens four more times during the night, every two hours. At dawn I hear her call once more, and I say to myself, "I can't do it. I can't go in there. I can't stand the anguish!" So what I do is I get up, walk fifteen feet of the thirty feet to her room, and stop. I can't go any further, yet she's calling me!

What do I do? I literally can't go on. I think, "Why doesn't she die so I don't have to deal with her pain anymore?" So then I realize, "My god, I just wished for the death of my wife!" And what do I do? I pray. I raise my arm and say, "Gentle Jesus, take my hand and help me see I'm forgiven for the thought that just crossed my mind. Please help me see I'm forgiven for wanting to kill my wife."

And instantly I get the peace. Because I really mean it, I get the peace. So now I'm able to go in, help my wife to the bathroom, and bring her back to her bed. And two more times there's the scream, but somehow I have a new strength and serenity about it. And this time after I lay my wife down, she puts her arms around me and says, "I'm so glad you're in my life."

That moment was a palpable demonstration of the miracle. I went from the hate of wanting to kill my wife, to this moment where real love and compassion were flowing between Martha and me. I went from hell to heaven, and it felt so good! And that's what you do; that's the process. You ask for Jesus' help (or the help of whomever you pray to) to heal the guilt that inevitably arises from the ego thought, which is without exception a thought of murder. Remember that the ego always speaks first; yet the Holy Spirit always answers, if you're open to hearing its answer. I was open to hearing the Holy Spirit that night outside Martha's bedroom, because how could I not go to her?

Q. Would you talk a little bit about separation, and how that idea originated in our minds, and how it's actually a false idea?

A. You're asking me to give the mythology behind the idea of separation. We have, for instance, the myth of the Garden of Eden. Every culture has a myth about the Beginning, which tries to explain why we are as we are; why we are as insane as we are. Well, the myth propounded by *A Course in Miracles*, the spiritual path that I follow—a path that, as I've told you, you don't have to believe in or subscribe to—goes something like this. The Course's view of separation is that we once were One, all of us joined in one undifferentiated state of Love. (In fact, according to the Course, we still are in this undifferentiated state of Love, dreaming, however, a nightmare of separation!)

And then (so goes the Course mythology) a tiny, mad idea crept into the mind of all of us at once (we were not individuals), the tiny, mad idea being that we could possibly be separate from Love. (Don't ask me how or why that idea came, because that's not answerable by me.) And somehow we forgot to laugh at the silliness of that idea. *I want power. I want my own individual way of running my life. I want, in short, to be God. I'm going to make a life of my own. I'm going to select the people in it. I'm going to have a life apart from God, apart from my Creator.* And it was as if a gigantic mirror that was our Oneness shattered in that instant[7], and each of us is a shard, identical to each other, but believing, mistakenly, that we are separate and different. We are different in terms of the form—female-male, old-young, black-white. But we're all the same in our essence, which is this (*points to right mind part of the drawing*). Separation is a wish for power, a wish for an identity of my own, a wish for specialness.

Specialness is something we all want. We want to be different from everybody else. I'll illustrate with a story from my own life. Every morning I take a two-mile walk, when the weather allows and I'm not lazy. I pick up trash because I like having a road that's clean. But sometimes when I bend down to pick up some trash and I see a car coming, I think, "Won't they think what a wonderful guy I am for picking this trash up?" (*Laughter*) Now that's specialness! I'm not the bad guy who throws the trash. I'm the special guy who picks up the trash. I'm different! We all want to be special. And I say to myself, "Frank, that's silly. Give that up." And then I pray. I say, "Gentle Jesus, take my hand and please help me see I'm forgiven for that silly thought that I need to be seen as wonderful, as special." That's my ego. That's the egotism that says, "Look at me. I'm hot stuff."

Q. *Why do bad things happen to good people?*

---

[7]　This metaphor was originally used by Gloria Wapnick.

A. Well, you may not believe this, but this is what I believe. I believe we *want* bad things to happen to us. We select it. It's like the patient I spoke of earlier who provoked her child to poke her in the eye. She set that up in order for something bad to happen because she was afraid and frightened of the love she'd been experiencing. That sounds weird, right? That's what we do. We're weird. But when you've put together a life based on the idea of separation, Love is perceived as a threat.

Something else I think we do. I believe that before we come here, we write a DVD script, the script of our life. And when we're born, we put that script in the DVD player, and we watch it happen. I believe this event here tonight I put in my script before I came to this planet, and it included all of you in it. And you put this same event in your script, and we have all come together at this moment. This event is, I believe, a good and helpful thing. But I have chosen some things that have not been cool for my life. And the reason I've chosen them is that either I wanted to have a lesson that I could learn to heal my mind this time around (I also believe in past lifetimes), or I came into this life with so much guilt I believe I deserve a miserable life. I know people who've done that. Their life is one misery after another, because of their guilt. And I'll ask them, "Why have you lived such a miserable life?" And I get the answer, "I deserve it." Then I say, "What do you mean you deserve it?" And they'll say, "Well, I did this and this and this when I was young, and now I have this hell to pay because of it." Now that's crazy! But we do crazy things. When we think we're bad, we find a way to be punished. We make punishment happen. Look at your life. Look clearly within. Don't look without, because the answer is not "out there." The answer is within your mind. This is why I love nightmares. I encourage my patients, "Please pray for a nightmare." They think I'm crazy, of course. They say, "Who wants a nightmare?" I say, "I do. And you do too, if you're in your right mind, because nightmares help you get acquainted with what's what in the depths of you, and what's in the depths is precisely what needs forgiving. That's why you want the nightmare."

Folks, you can't just plaster nice, sweet smiley faces over the ugliness. From my point of view, that's what the so-called New Age people try to do. It fails. It puts a temporary band-aid on a very corrosive cancer. You've got to see what needs forgiving, so that you can take it to the light of forgiveness, where it disappears. That's the process. You can't just make affirmation after affirmation, hoping against hope for some "positive" outcome, because that doesn't heal the darkness in your mind. That's why Freud was so wonderful. He has a bad press these days, but I'm glad I studied him, because he saw how dark the mind is. Unfortunately, he didn't know how to undo the darkness. He said his aim was—and I think I'm quoting him correctly—"to help the misery of hysteria become normal unhappiness." Now how's that for a cure? Hardly the good news I promised to bring to you tonight. Yet Freud really was a genius. The spiritual path I follow could not have been written without him, because it deals with the darkness. But Freud didn't know what to do with the darkness. Fortunately you do, having heard me speak tonight! (*Laughter*)

Q. Most of my hatred is directed at myself, and I want to get away from that because I think some of my health problems come from my anger and my anxiety. I suffer from ulcers, for instance.

A. I hear your guilt is causing you to attack your body. Do you have nightmares?

Q. No.

A. As I said before, nightmares let you know the nature of the hate you have. You're placid and smiling on the surface, but underneath there's a lot of hate, and the hate is directed at you. At your body.

So what I'd recommend—whenever you notice pain or discomfort in your body—is that you recall these words from the Course: "I am not my body. I am free, for I am still as God created me." The body, you see, is an ego construct. Yet the Holy Spirit can use the body (as it uses everything else) as a teaching tool.

I'll give you an example. I get my blood tested once a year as part of my annual checkup. A couple of years back they spotted something abnormal about my white blood cell count. So I was sent to a hematologist, who said, "Yes, I don't like it. We better do another test." She said she wanted to take some of my bone marrow.

Now I'd heard that the drawing-out of bone marrow is painful. So when I went for the procedure, I was prepared with the thought, *I am not my body. I am free, for I am still as God created me.* I kept repeating it to myself, like a mantra.

So I lay down on my belly, and a nurse stood over me with her hands held firmly on my upper back. That was to keep me still so I wouldn't writhe in pain and mess up what the hematologist was doing. She had a very big needle, and she gave me a local anesthetic before she plunged that needle into my hip bone. And right before she plunged it in, she said, "Now this is going to hurt." And then a little later, after the needle was in, she said again, "Be careful, this is going to hurt." Four or five times during the twenty minutes of the procedure she told me it was going to hurt. And do you know what? I had no pain whatsoever.

When it was over, the hematologist said to me, "I don't understand. You didn't seem to have any pain." And I said, "Do you want to know why?" Now remember I'm in a "body shop" with a body technician, who specializes in bodies! And I thought to myself, "Am I going to tell her the truth?" And I answered myself, "Yes, I'm going to tell her the truth." So I said to her, "Well, I was meditating." And she said, "You were?" And I said, "Do you want to know the form of my meditation?" She said, "Yes," and I thought, "Well, here goes." So I said to the doctor, "I was repeating over and over, *I am not a body. I am free, for I am still as God created me.*"[8]

---

[8]   *Workbook, ACIM, no. 199.*

I expected her to exclaim, "What do you mean, *not a body*?" She makes her living working on bodies! Instead she said, "Oh, what a wonderful statement. Let me get a pencil and write that down. Somebody else might be interested in that." Now how about that? I'd say that was a miracle, on top of the miracle of my deciding to remember who it is I really am. I chose to remember; that's all it is. We just keep on forgetting.[9] By the way, my white blood cells turned out to be just fine.

Q. I'd like to connect with a group studying A Course in Miracles. *What's the best way to do that?*

A. I would certainly encourage you to join a group. I'm particularly fond of Ken Wapnick, who heads up an organization in California called The Foundation for A Course in Miracles. His Web site is www.facim.org. He runs workshops out there, but he also travels and presents workshops in different parts of the country. I think he's brilliant. He really gets what the Course is all about, and for me, he's far and away the major teacher of the Course alive today. He was friends with Helen Schucman, who scribed the Course, and he helped her edit the original edition of the Course. So you might start with him or with people who have a connection with him. Also, if you log on to the Web site www.miraclecenter.org, you can find a listing of study groups by area code.

Ken also has a background in psychoanalysis, as do I. It was the psychology underlying the Course that first drew me to it. For years, I'd been yearning for an intellectually powerful mode of spirituality, and I found it in the Course. It's rigorous, it's uncompromising, and it's powerful. If you really get it, it frees your mind.

---

9   Another thing you can do when you are experiencing an attack on your body in the form of pain or illness is to search within for any guilt that may be related to that attack and that has in fact given rise to it.

I'm more at peace now than I've ever been. For example, a new patient recently joined one of my groups. He was dealing with a lot of depression. About the fourth group session he attended, he spent the first ten minutes of the session attacking me, accusing me of being selfish, autocratic, demanding, untrustworthy, and greedy. He said that all I was interested in was his money, because I charge for my therapy groups. He was accusing me of all kinds of crimes, right in front of the rest of the group. And I just sat there and listened. I listened to all this hate coming from him to me that I knew was his projection and that I recognized immediately as a cry for love. So I had no response of fear or hate in that moment. None whatsoever. And believe me when I tell you, that's a big change from how I would have responded ten or twenty years ago. That's a big change from the time when I attacked that deaf kid for running his stick along the bars of my apartment on Riverside Drive!

So in me you're looking at a walking billboard of how, thanks to the Course, my ego has been reduced. Not gone, mind you, because you will continue to hear the cry of the ego as long as you're here. But you will always make the correction when you're in the right mind to remember.

Q. *Do you have a favorite definition of "miracle?"*

A. Yes. The miracle is when an ancient hate is changed to a current love. That's the process. And it's done by forgiveness. It's not forgiveness for what you've done. It's forgiveness for what you *didn't* do. Now that's a curious statement, isn't it? For example, when my children were growing up, I acted in a way that I'm not proud of. But they were not hurt by the horror of my behavior. Their personalities were hurt. Only once I hit my son because he was mocking me, and I became enraged. And I struck him, and I was so guilty about that. But we are not our bodies, and we are not our personalities. We are this (*points to the drawing*), which is beyond body and beyond personality. That's the good news! So you can't really hurt a child, even though we do terrible things to children. But the child has this essence of Love that is not touched. That's the meaning of the Crucifixion and the Resurrection, by the way: Love cannot be hurt, not by anything. That's for those Christians who believe in that form, but I believe that Love is beyond all worldly things. It is an eternal state.

I describe in my book how four years ago Monday my wife died. I grieved for about a month, and then I began to get this tingling around my lips. I thought it was something neurological. I checked that out; it wasn't. The tingling kept happening three or four times a day. So I went to my psychic friend Ed Moret, and when I walked into his studio, he said, "My god, who is that woman with you with her arms around your neck, kissing your face? I think her name starts with an M. It's Mary or Madeleine—no no, she's telling me it's Martha. And she's telling me she's sorry you've been sad for the last month. But she wants you to know she's so grateful for the fifty-five years she was married to you." That blew me away. And then Ed told me, "She says she's going to be with you from now until the time you cross over, and will meet you and help you make your transition. And over the next eighteen months, she's going to help you move to another level spiritually." And Martha sure as hell has done that. My life has been radically changed since her death. I'm happier, more joyous, because—while I knew intellectually love never dies—now I know it in my heart, in my gut, through Martha's continued presence.

Bodies die. Worlds die. This house will go down into the ashes. But love never ever dies. Trust it. Any other questions?

Q. *Would you elaborate on the idea you mentioned earlier about forgiveness, that it's really about being forgiven for what you* didn't *do?*

A. I'll be glad to. I think Martha was the first person to teach me what forgiveness might really mean. I treated her badly at times. I was unfaithful to her on one occasion. I was often angry with her. But despite the attacks, despite the infidelity, somehow she saw that there was nothing there that really hurt her. She didn't hold onto a grievance about me. And that's what I encountered when I visited my psychic friend, when through him I heard Martha say, "I'm so grateful for the fifty-five years I was married to you, and I will be with you for the rest of your life."

So I'm saying that once you think something happened that was hurtful, you're stuck with guilt. If you really want the peace, you must live at this level (*points to the right mind part of the drawing*), up here, and not down here where bad things happen between people that affect bodies and personalities. It is hard for us to get the idea that we're not our personality or our body. It helps to remember that a basic teaching of the Course is that the world is an illusion, and only love is real. And love is real because it never changes. It is eternal.

Q. Through reading A Course in Miracles, *and your book as well, I'm more and more sure that the things that have bothered me the most in my life are fear and guilt. And at the ripe old age of—well, never mind how old I am!—I'm realizing that all my life I've been afraid of things that I have no reason to fear. Like when, as a young woman, I had an abortion, and feeling the fear that my parents would find out, and also the awful guilt that I had done something terrible. And the* Course *and your book are helping me start to see that there's no reason for that.*

A. Well, thank you. Let me see if I've understood you correctly. You are saying that all your life you have been afflicted with guilt and fear. And this has caused you anguish. And what has helped you lately is reading *A Course in Miracles* (which you've studied for some time, as I recall), and also my book, for which I'm grateful. And these books have enabled you, to some degree, to lift that guilt and free your mind from fear. Did I get that right?

Q. Yes. Thank you.

A. You're welcome! Any other questions?

Q. As you know, there has been a lot of focus recently on the year 2012 and how that year is supposed to be one of great transformation, a transformation of some kind within the general consciousness of the planet. *Do you have any thoughts on that with regard to the Course?*

A. You're asking me whether I have any understanding of the supposed raising of general consciousness in the year 2012 to a higher level of—I'm using these terms—love and peace?

Q. No.

A. No? I'm sorry. Well, to "higher consciousness" then. Excuse me for putting words in your mouth! Whether that will happen in 2012 . . . I really don't know. I would hope so, because we need a raising of consciousness!

The Course's view is that the world is a loony bin. It's Ward 8, Bellevue. And we're all running around insane. I hope we get some sense into us in 2012, or in any year. I do know that the view of the Course is that it's the healing of one mind at a time that contributes to the healing of all. There are those who predict great physical and mental turmoil for 2012 and thereafter. I know nothing about that. But what I do know is that preparing our minds to experience peace will be of great help, should those predictions come to pass.

Q. I find it very useful to get in touch with my needs and feelings before I can get to what's truly going on inside—then I know what I have to forgive. What is your process of forgiveness?

A. I'm so glad to hear that you've learned the essential truth that looking within is the beginning of wisdom. But as you say, it is only the beginning.

When I really want the peace forgiveness brings, the steps I take are these:

First, I ask myself, "Am I in enough pain (as a result of the insane self-hate I've chosen) to really want to see I have another choice?" You see, I've *really* got to desire intensely to seek freedom from the ego trap I've chosen, or else the process will merely be an empty ritual with no meaning.

The second step, then, is simple. I cry for help, because I know I can't do this alone. The particular form I use is to ask for the help of Jesus—that he take my hand and help me look at myself the way he does that is, with a kind and gentle smile. I imagine his smiling at my silliness for having made the mistake of projecting my self-hate onto my holy brother or sister *or holy Self* and thereby choosing the illusion of separation. And instantly, *if I've really meant it,* I receive the peace of His Love.

Q. When a person trespasses against us, how do we get from overlooking, or simply forgetting, the trespass, to actually expressing forgiveness?

A. This question mirrors the last one. But it gives me the chance to address the illusory idea that we've actually been hurt by any "trespass" against us. Whenever we think we've been hurt or unfairly treated, we are simply making the mistake of perceiving that the essence of what we are is either our physical body or our psychological body. We have merely forgotten we are the Holy Sons of God, incapable of injury. Jesus says in his Course: "I am not mistaken. Your mind will elect to join with mine, and together we are invincible" (*T-4.IV.11:4, 5*).

With that awareness in your mind, it is no longer a matter of "forgetting" or "overlooking." The truth is that *nothing has happened.* Only love is real. If the experience was not of love, then it is nothing more than the smoke and mirrors of this illusory world. Jesus says in another place, "You cannot be unfairly treated. The belief you are is but another form of the idea you are deprived by someone not yourself . . . You have no enemy except yourself" (*T-26.X.3:2, 3, 6*)

When you have seen that you have merely perceived your brother and yourself incorrectly, and you remember the ideas I just quoted, you will not "express forgiveness." There is nothing to forgive! In that moment, you and your brother are joined. In that moment, your light has shined on him and has called forth the light in him. A sense of deep gratitude follows as a consequence of that joining (*T-13.VI.10, 11*). You have chosen the atonement for yourself, and the result is peace.

Q. What is the difference between attacking another and authentically expressing a feeling of sadness or anger in relationship with a loved one?

A. An attack upon a brother is nothing but a projection of our guilt, or self-hate, onto him. It is thus a deluded attempt to cling to an illusion of innocence for ourselves at the expense of our brother. Attack is only a desperate cry for love, an anguished cry of pain (this applies also to any perceived "attack" upon us by someone else).

As to expressing your sadness or anger as a consequence of some disappointment with a loved one: whether these expressions constitute an attack or not depends on the *content* of your mind. The Course is always urging us to ask ourselves about anything we do, "What is its purpose? What is it for?"

Expressing our sadness or our feelings of anger are behaviors, that is, *forms* in the illusion. It's not the form that's important. What's important is the *content* of our mind that initiates the behavior.

For example, if in your sadness or anger you can remember that, as Jesus says in the Course, "you have no enemy except yourself," you may be able to describe your sadness or anger to your loved one in a way that acknowledges that your feelings are the consequence of a mistaken and insane belief, the belief that you, as a holy son of God, could possibly be hurt. You might then choose to ask your loved one's forgiveness for your mistaken state of mind, remembering, of course, that his forgiveness is not for *you,* but rather for *him.* This would then give your brother the opportunity to make a choice loving to himself.

You, on the other hand, actually need no forgiveness, for you have remembered that forgiveness has already been given to both you and your brother at your creation. Again, there is nothing to forgive. That is one of the Course's most radical ideas.

Expressing your sadness or anger in any other state of mind would, of course, arise from your choosing to listen to the wrong side of your mind, that is, the ego. The content of *anything* we express can only be *either* fear or love. One or the other. Never both. So I would ask you, in all you do or say, to try to be more aware of the *content,* the *purpose* behind any given behavior. (By the way, folks, I understand that these ideas may be hard for you to get your heads around. That's okay. I just ask that you think about what I've said, and test it for yourselves.)

Chapter 6

Benediction

By way of closing, I'm going to read you a final meditation from *A Course in Miracles*. As you know, "light" is equivalent to "love'" in this spiritual path, as it is in many spiritual paths.

Child of light you know not that the light is in you yet you will find it through its witnesses. For having given light to them they will return it. Each one you see in light brings your light closer to your awareness. Love always leads to love. The sick who ask for love are grateful for it and in their joy they shine with holy thanks, and this they offer you who gave them joy. They are your guides to joy, for having received it of you they would keep it. You have established them as guides to peace, for you have made it manifest in them. And seeing it, its beauty calls you home.

There is a light in this world that the world cannot give. Yet you can give it as it was given you. And as you give it, it shines forth to call you from the world and follow it. For this light will attract you as nothing in the world can do. And you will lay aside the world and find another. This other world is bright with love which you have given it. And here will everything remind you of your Father and His holy Son. Light is unlimited, and spreads across this world in quiet joy. All those you brought with you will shine on you, and you will shine on them in gratitude because they brought you here. Your light will join with theirs in power so compelling that it will draw the others out of darkness as you look on them. (T-13.VI.10, 11)

Thank you very much.

About The Author

Frank West has practiced psychotherapy and family counseling for over fifty years. He holds a master's degree in divinity from the Union Theological Seminary in New York, where he specialized in the psychology of religion. He completed his graduate and postgraduate studies in psychology at the American Foundation of Religion and Psychiatry, the William Alanson White Institute, the City College of New York, and the Nathan Ackerman Institute for Family Therapy. Frank served as lecturer and supervisor in both psychoanalysis and marital/family therapy at the Blanton-Peale Institute, the Union Theological Seminary, and the Millhauser Research Laboratory at NYU Medical Center. He maintained a private psychotherapy practice in Manhattan for twenty-five years before relocating his practice to Guilford, Connecticut, in 1984. Soon after moving to Connecticut, he and his late wife, Martha, began studying *A Course in Miracles*, whose psychospiritual precepts have since become the cornerstone of his work with patients. Frank is a member of the American Association of Marriage and Family Therapists, and a founding member of the American Association of Pastoral Counselors. He continues to maintain a full schedule of private and group therapy patients.

Edwards Brothers,Inc!
Thorofare, NJ 08086
01 July, 2010
BA2010182